EXPLORING OUR WORLD:

Neighborhoods and Communities

Activities • Map & Model Projects • Literature Links

Kathleen M. Hollenbeck

SCHOLASTIC
PROFESSIONAL **B**OOKS

New York ❀ Toronto ❀ London ❀ Auckland ❀ Sydney

To Alex, Kyle, and Kelsie
who make my neighborhood a brighter place.

Cover design by Jaime Lucero and Vincent Ceci
Interior design by Jaime Lucero for Grafica, Inc.
Cover and interior illustrations by Paige Billin-Frye

ISBN 0-590-89809-4

Table of Contents

INTRODUCTION

Welcome to **Exploring Our World: Neighborhoods and Communities.** The literature-based and hands-on activities in this resource will provide your students with lots of opportunities to discover their surroundings. As they learn about the people and places within their communities, they will also build on the concepts of cooperation, living with diversity and change, and making a personal contribution for the common good.

The book is organized into four parts. Part One introduces the people and places found in neighborhoods and communities through literature, observation, games, and activities. In Part Two, students create community models and maps, and begin to build an understanding of the relationship between the real world and maps. The way communities grow and change is explored in Part Three. Finally, in Part Four, students explore an individual's contributions to neighborhood and community, and also learn how each of them can make a difference.

Throughout the guide, students develop their map-reading skills, explore their place in a larger environment, and discover the benefits of being sensitive to the concerns of their neighbors and community.

You don't need to do the activities in sequence. You can pick and choose those activities that best meet the needs and interests of your students. Suggestions are often given for adapting activity ideas for older or younger students. The range of activity types—from listening to books to creating models to charting students' observations—will capture the interest of students of all learning styles.

Enjoy your explorations!

USING THE POSTER

Bound in the back of the book is a poster. To get the most from your poster, use it both for display and for hands-on activities in the classroom.

Use the poster for display: Hang the poster in a prominent spot in your room where students will have easy access to it. Use it as an aid when discussing different locations within a community and various aspects of community life, such as buying food, growing food, delivering mail, traveling to and from work and school, and so on. Ask each student to choose one location on the poster and write/dictate a story that involves that location. Encourage students to feature other community locations in their stories as well.

Use the poster as a hands-on teaching tool. Place the poster on a large table. On page 31 are illustrations of people and vehicles that students can color and cut out, and then move around on the poster. Show students how to make the figures stand upright by taping the bottom flap to a coin or a square of cardboard.

As students move around the neighborhood:

🏠 Invite students to move the characters and vehicles around the poster in imaginary play. You might want to encourage them to enact situations that arise in a community, such as people pitching in to build a playground or deciding what to do to stop pets from running loose around town.

Have students take turns making up riddles to lead classmates to various points on the poster. For example, when directing a classmate to a convenience store or supermarket, a student might say: "You won't find a cow here, but you will find plenty of milk!"

Ask them to follow directions, such as, "Drive to the playground. Then go to the post office." Invite them to make up directions for each other.

Point out the compass rose. Then give students directions using the words north, south, east, and west. For example, you could say, "Start at the school. Then go 2 blocks east. Where are you?"

What Are neighborhoods and Communities?

Part 1

I n Part One, students develop a greater awareness of their surroundings by first observing and exploring the neighborhood around school, and then expanding their explorations to include their community.

INTRODUCING NEIGHBORHOODS

My Perfect Neighborhood by Leah Komaiko. (HarperCollins, 1990)
Reading Leah Komaiko's *My Perfect Neighborhood* is a great way to introduce children to the concept of neighborhood. In the story, a young girl describes her own neighborhood, embellishing her view of it to an amusing extent.

Before Reading
Hold the book so students can see the front cover. Invite them to guess where the story takes place (a city neighborhood). Ask students to identify the things on the front cover that tell them the story happens in a neighborhood.

After Reading
Talk about the neighborhood described in the story. Ask students to tell which of the sights are make-believe and which they might really find in a neighborhood. Invite children to tell you what they liked best in the "perfect" neighborhood. Have students compare the neighborhood in the story to their own neighborhood. *How are they the same? How are they the different?* Invite students to share their ideas with the class. For example, the neighborhood in *My Perfect Neighborhood* is set in a city where there are many stores and restaurants nearby. If your students live in a city, they may also have such establishments on their block. Children who live in a rural community, however, may describe the homes and/or farms in their neighborhood.

Extension Activities

1. Make a Chart You may want to make a chart to separate the real and make-believe sights in the neighborhood.

2. Imagine a Perfect Neighborhood Help students brainstorm in small groups or as a class to create a list of attributes they would find in a "perfect" neighborhood. Examples might include: purple streets, ice cream stands on every corner, hopscotch and shuffleboard games painted on every sidewalk, a slide next to every set of stairs, and so on. Have each student draw his/her own version of the perfect neighborhood, prompted by the brainstorming session. Display the finished drawings on a bulletin board labeled "Our Perfect Neighborhoods."

Make-Believe	Real
dogs waving	apartment buildings
brick-cream pie	stores
poodle in wedding dress	sidewalks
horse on skates	restaurants

What's in a Neighborhood? A Mini-Book

Supplies: Copies of page 16 for each child, scissors, crayons, and markers.

Invite children to make a mini-book that tells about a neighborhood. Show students how to cut out the book and the four word boxes. Show them how to fold the book in half lengthwise, and then in half again to make a book. (See the diagram.) Then ask them to match the word boxes to the correct page in the book and paste the boxes in. On the last page of the book, they should write or dictate to you the name of their community and write it on the "Welcome" sign. Then have them color their mini-books.

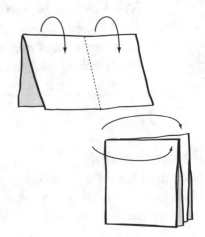

Neighborhood Walk

Give children a chance to use their observational skills by going on a walking tour of their school neighborhood. Ask students to carefully observe the buildings and places they see as they walk. When you return to the classroom, make a simple graph using chart paper and sticky notes on which you write or have children write their names. Put the notes alongside the places observed, as shown on the next page.

What We Saw in the Neighborhood	How Many Students Saw It				
Post Office	Rick	Tanya	Liza	Tim	Terri
Apartment Building	Tony	Liza	Juan		
Church	Liza				
Pond	Tim	Jaime	Terri		
Playground	Tony	Terri			

Extension Activities

1. A Five Senses Mini-Book Link science and social studies by having students record the sounds, smells, tastes, and "touches" in their neighborhood. Show them how to fold a blank piece of paper in half lengthwise, and then in half again. (As they did with the Neighborhood mini-book.) Have them illustrate each page with something they saw, heard, and touched on one page each. On the last page they can illustrate something they smelled or tasted. Display their mini-books in the classroom.

2. A Neighborhood Poem Invite students to write a poem about their neighborhood. Encourage them to use the places they observed in their neighborhood walk in the poem. You may want to read aloud the poem "My Neighborhood" (see box) to get them thinking.

My Neighborhood

My neighborhood is old, it seems.
The sidewalks all are cracked.
The houses stand together,
Side by side and back to back.
The lawns are small and weedy
With little grass at all
And evergreens I cannot climb
Because they are so tall.

My neighborhood is old, it seems.
The sidewalks all are cracked.
My friends and I jump over them
And back across and back.
My friends live in the houses
Behind and next to mine.
My lawn's just right for kickball.
My swing hangs from a pine.

—Kathleen M. Hollenbeck

Different Kinds of Neighborhoods

BOOKSTOP

The Town Mouse and the Country Mouse by Lorinda Bryan Cauley
(G. P. Putnam, 1984)
Neighborhoods, as your students have probably already observed, are not all alike. Reading this book with your students is a great way to begin discussing different kinds of neighborhoods and of introducing students to the concepts of urban and rural.

Before Reading

Ask students to describe a city neighborhood, telling what they might see there. List their descriptions on the chalkboard. Then ask students to describe a neighborhood in the country. Again, list their descriptions. Explain that there is also another type of neighborhood that is between the city and the country and is a little bit like both: a suburban neighborhood. Help students determine in which kind of neighborhood they live. Then explain that today's story will tell about life in a city and in the country.

After Reading

Talk with students about the way each mouse felt about the other mouse's home. Help students understand that neither the city nor the country is a better place to live, yet both mice felt most comfortable in their own homes because they knew what to expect and enjoy there. Each type of neighborhood had many good things to offer, and each held many dangers as well.

Extension Activities

1. Put on a Puppet Show Invite the class to use the mice on the reproducible on page 17 to retell the story. They may want to create scenery for the puppet show by drawing pictures that show the country and the city.

2. A Neighborhood Sort Ask children to find pictures of neighborhoods in old magazines that they can cut out. After you've collected at least 25 pictures, encourage children to sort them. Tell them they can sort them any way they like as long as they can give reasons for their choices. You may also take a turn at sorting, and sort the pictures into 3 groups: urban, rural, and suburban. Explain what clues in the pictures helped you decide how to sort.

INTRODUCING COMMUNITIES

Once students become familiar with the concept of a neighborhood and what might be found in it, they can expand that knowledge to a group of neighborhoods or a *community*. These fun, interactive activities reinforce the concept of community and increase students' awareness of what is available in their own community.

An A-MAZE-ing Community

Supplies: Copies of page 18 for each student, pencils

In this activity, students trace a route through an AMAZING community and learn about various places in the community and the reasons that families frequent them.

Have students follow the directions on page 18 to trace the route. Younger students can trace the route as you read the directions aloud to them.

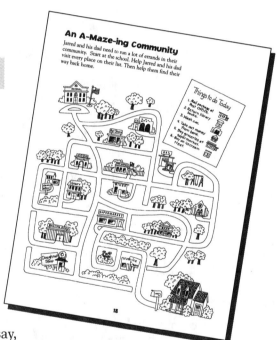

Extension Activities

1. Community Clues Call on student volunteers to describe places in their community as classmates try to guess each location. For example, a student might say, "An American flag flies in front of this building, and there are large blue boxes on the sidewalk in front of it." For younger students, a clue for the same location might be, "People go here to mail letters."

2. Alphabet Community Have students sit in a circle to play an alphabet game that will teach them about places in a community. Begin the game by saying aloud one place in a community that begins with the letter A, such as airport. Go around the circle, with each student in turn naming a place for the letter that comes next. (Examples include: A: aquarium; B: bookstore; C: church; Z: zoo.)

3. Community Yellow Pages Have students brainstorm as a class or in small groups to create a list of places in their community where people go to buy, rent, or borrow things they need. Examples include stores, restaurants, the library, pet shops, beauty salons, and so on. Explain that these places provide goods and services people need or want. Ask if these places are found in the students' own neighborhoods, or if they must travel to a different neighborhood to find them.

Provide each group with yellow lined paper and ask them to write out their own "yellow pages," organizing their list of places by category such as food, clothing, etc. Then show students the real thing: an actual telephone book with yellow pages for their community. Allow time for students to browse through the phone book, adding to their own yellow pages as they wish. The main idea here is not to include every establishment in the book, but rather to give students a general idea of the types and variety of goods and services available in their community. Younger students may wish to choose between one and five favorite places in the community and illustrate themselves (eating/shopping/playing) there.

Where in the Community?

Supplies: Copies of pages 19-21, dice, coins or small squares of paper

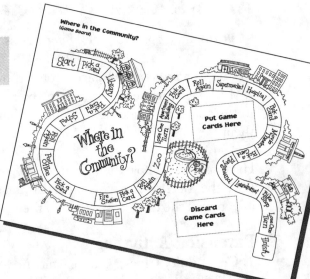

In this fun riddle game, students explore all that a community can provide. Students may want to make their own game cards and boards, then laminate them.

How To Play the Game:
1. Divide the class into small groups. Give each group one copy of page 19, 20, and 21 as well as one die. Have them cut out the cards and place them on the game board.

2. Using coins or colored squares of paper for tokens, have each player place his/her token on the space marked "START." Each player in turn rolls the die and moves that number of spaces. Players travel around the board, moving forward and back as directed by cards and spaces. The first player to land on FINISH by exact count wins the game.

3. When a player lands on PICK A CARD, s/he must pick a card and read the riddle aloud (for younger students you should read the riddles aloud to them). The player must identify and move his/her playing piece to the location described.

Extension Activities
1. Make Extra Cards Provide students with white paper and have them make extra cards for the board game. Encourage them to write their own riddles about the places they see.

2. Label the Places Have your students label the game board with the actual names of places in their community. For example, they might write the name of their school as well as the name of a popular supermarket or movie theater. In the blank space, ask students to draw and label an additional establishment, such as their home or a store.

3. Make Personalized Tokens. Give each student one sheet from a miniature-sized adhesive memo pad. Have students draw themselves on the sheet, and then fold it at the bottom and stick it to a piece of cardboard so the figure stands upright. Students can use these as their playing pieces and move "themselves" around the board.

Community Helpers

Supplies: copies of page 22 for each child, paper fasteners, crayons or markers, scissors

In this activity, children create a fact wheel to help them explore the variety of jobs and services in a community. Copy page 22 and distribute one copy to each student. Direct students to assemble the wheel as follows:

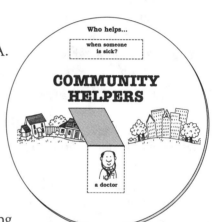

1. Cut out the wheels along the dark lines.
2. Cut out the windows along the dashed lines on wheel A. Fold along the solid line on the bottom window to create a "flap."
3. Place wheel A on top of wheel B, and connect them with a paper fastener.
4. As students turn the wheel, have them guess which worker is being described before they lift the flap.

Extension Activities

1. Mini-Center on Community Workers Create a learning center about community workers. Draw or cut from a magazine pictures of various community workers. Have students paste each picture on a separate index card, then flip the card over and write or dictate to you the name of the worker's job and a brief description of what it entails. In the center, students can either create the cards or, using those already made, can sort them according to profession (medical, education, sales, etc.). Older students familiar with community concepts may also be able to sort based on whether the worker provides goods or services.

2. Community Jobs Invite students to apply to you for jobs that are common in most communities, such as mail carrier, retail store clerk, and so on. Students should first brainstorm to come up with job titles, then apply for the jobs and tell why they feel the job is important and why they would make a worthy candidate for the position. Extend the activity by having students interact in their assigned roles, buying/selling goods and using/providing services. NOTE: This activity will require some research to determine the real-life responsibilities associated with each job.

3. Who Am I? Pantomime with a professional touch! Have students take turns acting out the roles of doctor, teacher, farmer, and people in various other professions while classmates guess their identities.

Communities Far Away

Rehema's Journey: A Visit to Tanzania by Barbara A. Margolis (Scholastic, 1990)

It's easy to focus on everyday life in one's own community. *Rehema's Journey* and the extension activities that follow help broaden your students' understanding of and appreciation for communities far away from their own. By reading this book about a girl in Tanzania, students can learn about the way of life in this African country.

Before Reading

Ask students to find their community on a globe. Help students name the country in which they live and the continent on which their country is located. Explain that today you will read a story about a girl who lives in the country of Tanzania, which is on the opposite side of the world in Africa. In this story, students will accompany Rehema as she travels from her mountain home for the first time.

Tanzania

After Reading

On the chalkboard or on chart paper, make a simple three-column chart. Above the left column, write "Chores and Activities." Above the middle column, write "Rehema and Her Community." Above the right column, write "Our Community." Invite students to study the photos in the book and note the chores and activities that are the same in Rehema's community and in their community. Then ask students how those chores and activities are done differently in their community. Write each observation on the chart as students name it. (See sample chart.)

Chores and Activities	Rehema and Her Community	Our Community
Shopping		Supermarket

1. Make Your Own Books Invite each student to write and illustrate a book about a trip he or she took. Explain that it can be a trip anywhere: to a zoo, a department store, or a relative's house. Encourage them to include information such as how they traveled, what they saw, what they liked, and how they felt at the end of their journey. Display the books in the classroom.

2. One Way to Travel Provide one copy of Anita Lobel's *Away from Home* (Greenwillow, 1994), in which 26 children are depicted at famous sites around the world. Assign pairs or small groups a number of sites from the book and ask them to locate the country of origin on a globe or map of the world. The groups might draw and label small pictures of the sites and fashion them to the appropriate countries on the map or globe using sticky notes.

Bookshelf

Neighborhoods and Communities

The American Family Farm by George Ancona (Harcourt Brace Jovanovich, 1989) This photo essay depicts life on three family farms, in Georgia, Iowa, and Massachusetts.

The Magic School Bus at the Waterworks by Joanna Cole (Scholastic, 1986) Ms. Frizzle takes her class on an exciting adventure from a rain cloud to the community waterworks.

Family Pictures by Carmen Lomas Garza (Children's Book Press, 1990) The author fondly remembers her childhood in a Texas community near the Mexican border.

Farming by Gail Gibbons (Holiday House, 1988) Bold illustrations present the many details of life on and around a farm.

Nighttime on Neighborhood Street by Eloise Greenfield (Dial Books for Young Readers, 1991) Families and friends celebrate life and togetherness in the evening.

The Night Ones by Patricia Grossman (Harcourt Brace Jovanovich, 1991) While others settle down for a good night's sleep, the night bus brings a variety of workers to their night shifts in the city.

Once Around the Block by Kevin Henkes (Greenwillow, 1987) Annie is bored, so she walks around her neighborhood, finding pleasant surprises along the way.

One Afternoon by Yumi Heo (Orchard Books, 1994) Minho spends a day running errands with his mother. From laundromat to supermarket, readers catch a glimpse of his city.

Neighborhood Odes by Gary Soto (Harcourt Brace Jovanovich, 1992) Through poetry, the author conveys the sights and sounds of a Mexican-American neighborhood.

Communities Far Away

The Village of Round and Square Houses by Ann Grifalconi (Little, Brown and Company, 1986) In the African village of Tos, women live in round houses and men in square ones.

Tonight Is Carnaval by Arthur Dorros (Dutton Children's Books, 1991) A young boy in Peru helps his family prepare for the exciting festival called Carnaval.

The Day of Ahmed's Secret by Florence Parry Heide and Judith Heide Gilliland (Lothrop, Lee & Shepard, 1990) All day long as he works in the city of Cairo, young Ahmed waits to share an exciting secret with his family.

Over the Green Hills by Rachel Isadora (Greenwillow, 1992) A boy and his mother travel the South African countryside to reach his grandmother's home, seeing villagers and sights along the way.

Children Just Like Me by Barnabas and Anabel Kindersley (Dorling Kindersley, 1995) Readers meet children in countries around the world, learning much about their families, friends, daily lives, likes and dislikes, clothing, food, homes, and more. Exquisite photos, quotes from the children themselves, and minute details bring each child's world to life.

Springtime in Noisy Village by Astrid Lindgren (Viking, 1966) Children in a Swedish village welcome spring.

All About Things People Do by Melanie and Chris Rice (Doubleday, 1990) Around the world, people hold a variety of jobs. Bus drivers, factory workers, chefs, and athletes are among the many who work each day.

What's in a Neighborhood?
(*A Mini-Book*)

fold here

fold here

Welcome to

(name of your community here)

SCHOOL

FIRE · HOUSE

Pets

Neighborhoods

Neighborhoods have people.

Neighborhoods have homes.

Neighborhoods have names.

Neighborhoods have places to shop, work, and learn.

cut here

Town Mouse and Country Mouse Puppets

Color and cut out the puppets. Glue them to a craft stick. Then retell the story about the town mouse and country mouse.

An A-Maze-ing Community

Jarred and his dad need to run a lot of errands in their community. Start at the school. Help Jarred and his dad visit every place on their list. Then help them find their way back home.

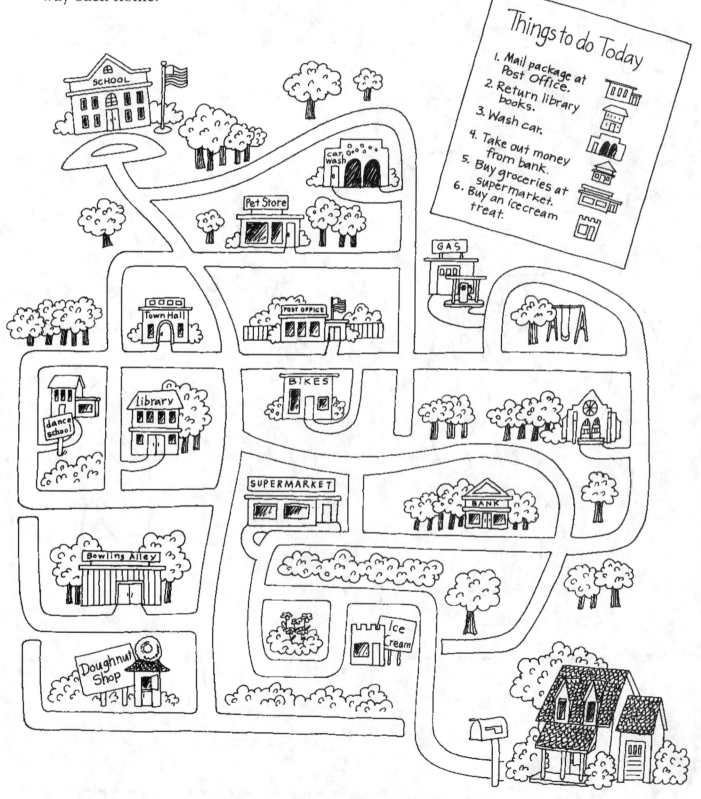

Things to do Today

1. Mail package at Post Office.
2. Return library books.
3. Wash car.
4. Take out money from bank.
5. Buy groceries at supermarket.
6. Buy an ice cream treat.

You fell down and broke a bone.
Now what will you do?
Ask a friend to bring you here.
You'll be good as new!

Smell the hot and spicy foods,
With cheese or without.
Hunger won't last long in here.
Eat here or take out.

Sunny day! You want to run
And do outdoor things.
Find a place with jungle gyms,
Slides, seesaws, and swings.

Clothes are dirty? Piling up?
Bring your basket here.
Wash and dry and fold your clothes.
Dirt will disappear!

Buy your ticket. Take a seat.
Watch the giant screen.
Movie stars seem close and real
When they're in this scene.

Tired of walking everywhere?
Why not try a bike?
Here we have a lot to see.
Which one do you like?

Lions roar and owls hoot.
Monkeys laugh and climb.
Come to see the animals.
Have a wild time!

All across the countryside,
All throughout the year,
Letters, packages, and such
Start their travels here.

Workers here are on the go.
Traveling all about.
When a fire starts, they help
Put the fire out.

Books on dragonflies and bees,
Books on cats and elves,
Books on anything at all
Fill up all the shelves.

Hungry for some cereal?
Want some fruit instead?
Buy the food you need right here.
Don't forget the bread!

Morning till mid-afternoon,
Here's the place to be;
Learning everything you can;
Counting 1 - 2 - 3!

19

Where in the Community?
(Game Board)

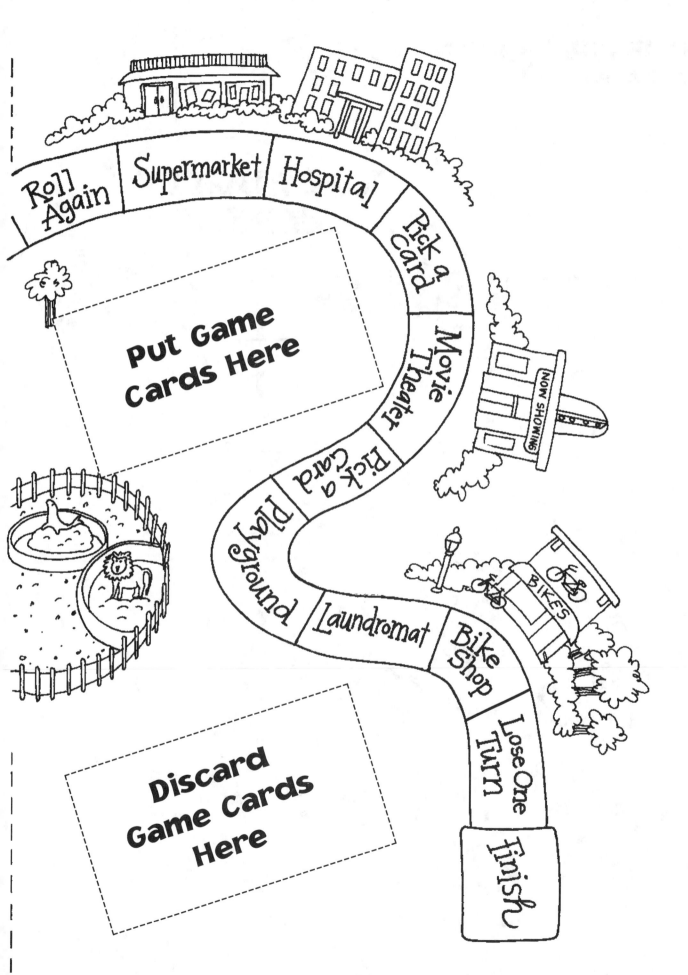

Roll Again

Supermarket

Hospital

Pick a Card

Movie Theater

NOW SHOWING

Pick a Card

Playground

Laundromat

Bike Shop

BIKES

Lose One Turn

Finish

Put Game Cards Here

Discard Game Cards Here

Community Helpers
(Fact Wheel)

Wheel A

Who helps...

COMMUNITY HELPERS

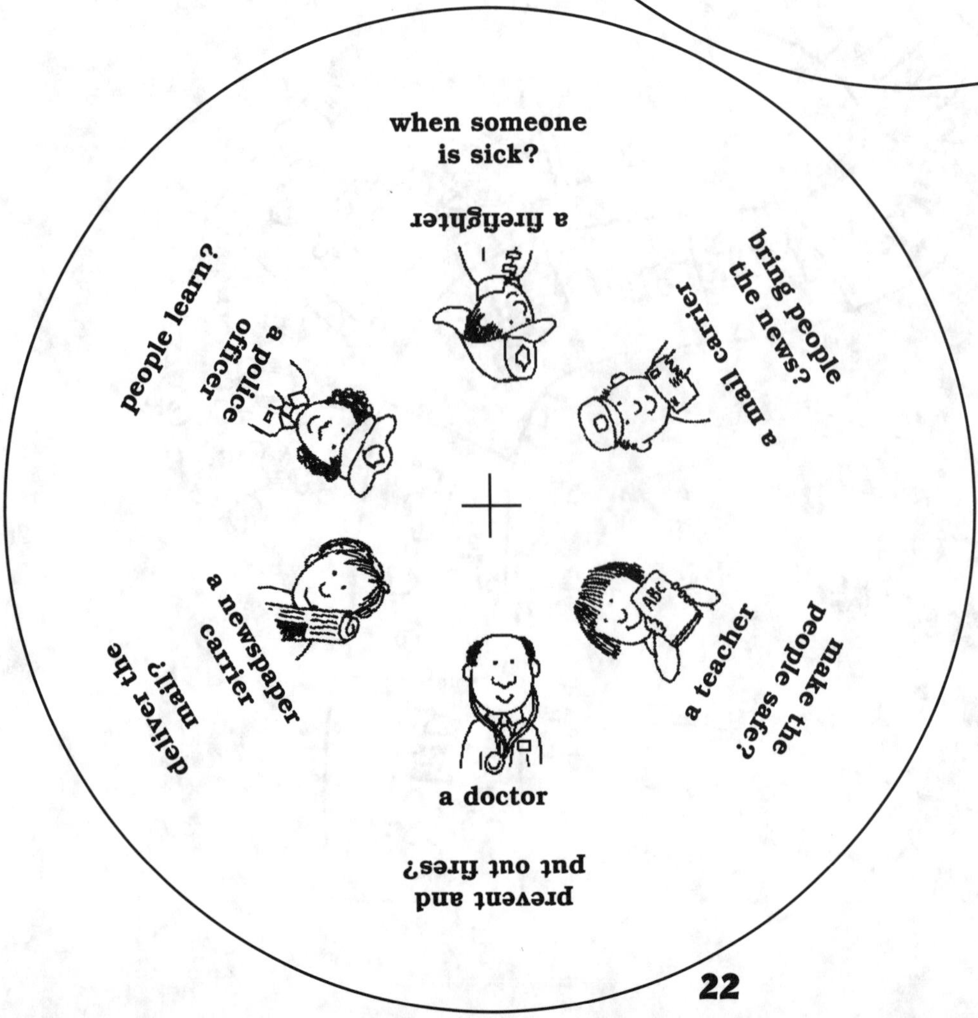

+

?

Wheel B

when someone is sick?

a firefighter

bring people the news?

a mail carrier

people learn?

a police officer

+

make the people safer?

a teacher

a newspaper carrier

deliver the mail?

a doctor

prevent and put out fires?

Models
and Maps

Part
2

Learning about neighborhoods and communities is a natural way to introduce models and maps. Reading and using maps can be difficult for some children. By starting with models you can provide a concrete, hands-on starting point for introducing maps. Models also give students a chance to explore different perspectives. Developing an understanding of the perspective represented in a map becomes easier when students have an actual model to which they can compare a map.

MODELS

Roxaboxen by Alice McLerran (Lothrop, Lee & Shepard, 1991)
Making models is an exciting and fun way for children to learn about neighborhoods and communities. This fanciful story will boost your students' imagination, and inspire them to create their own make-believe town.

Before Reading
Hold up the book and ask students to look at its cover. Invite them to tell what the children are doing and what they think the story might be about.

After Reading
Talk with students about the idea that Roxaboxen was a make-believe village, created by children for fun, yet it also had many of the components of a real-life village: stores, homes, traffic rules and regulations, and so on. Share with students the information on the very last page of the book, which informs readers that the make-believe village of Roxaboxen did indeed exist for children in Yuma, Arizona, many years ago. (The author's mother was one of the creators of Roxaboxen.)

Divide the class into small groups. Provide each group with a large rectangle of heavy cardboard, and art supplies such as glue, sand, small rocks, twigs, and clear beads. Have each group design their own "Roxaboxen," gluing the art supplies onto the cardboard to indicate the position of homes, stores, restaurants, and more in their imaginary towns.

Extension Activities

1. An Imaginary Village Read *Our Village* by John Yeoman and Quentin Blake (Atheneum, 1988), a collection of poems recalling olden-day life in a make-believe village. After reading the book, have students write and illustrate their own poems or stories involving fictitious characters and communities.

2. Onscreen Villages Brainstorm with your students to name imaginary communities featured on children's television programs or movies. For example, younger students might choose Pooh Corner, Mister Rogers' Neighborhood, Sesame Street, and the undersea world of Disney's Little Mermaid. Talk about features that the communities have in common, such as homes for the characters, places for keeping one's things, places for meeting and eating, and so on.

3. Find Yuma, Arizona, on a Map Help students locate Yuma, Arizona, where Roxaboxen was created years ago.

4. Travel the U.S. Urge students to bring in picture books and chapter books set in real places in the United States. Each time you or a student shares one with the class, have students look on a map and mark the location where the story took place. Try to "visit" as many locations in the U.S. as possible during the school year. Talk about similarities and differences from one place to another.

A 3-D Model Community

> **Supplies:** copies of the reproducibles on pages 31-34; several of the following empty containers: 8.45 oz. juice boxes, toaster pastries boxes, and 1/2 pint milk cartons; scissors; and paste or clear tape

Give students hands-on experience in arranging and working with communities by providing them with their own 3-dimensional models.

1. Divide the class into small groups.

2. Reproduce pages 31-34, and give each group copies of the pages. Have group members cut out the models of the homes, buildings, people, and vehicles and color them. Then show students how to paste the completed building models to empty containers as suggested below:

juice box (home, store, or other small building)
toaster pastries box (apartment building or other large structure)
milk carton (house)

The people and vehicle figures will stand upright if the bottom tab is taped to a coin or a square of cardboard.

3. Provide each group with a large sheet of craft paper. Ask them to spread the paper flat on the floor and draw the landscape on which they will place their models. Landscapes might include streets, grassy areas, ponds or lakes, parking lots and other paved areas, and so on. NOTE: You may wish to provide younger students with a pre-fab neighborhood rug or help them place masking tape on the floor or carpet to serve as roads.

4. Allow students to arrange and rearrange their neighborhood during free time. Encourage students to explain their communities. Why did they include what they did? Why did they locate buildings where they did?

Extension Activities

1. Which View? Divide the class into five different groups. Ask members of each group to draw pictures of their model from different viewpoints: one group for each of its four sides, and one group using a "bird's eye" view—from above. Help students to compare the drawings by displaying them by group on a bulletin board. Discuss the differences in the drawings. Encourage students to see that the "bird's eye" view drawings are the ones that most completely show the model. Explain that maps are "bird's eye" view drawings of different places on earth.

Working in Groups

Before students begin making models, take the time to reinforce the basics of working in groups:

1. Everyone counts. All group members should be encouraged to share ideas and skills to complete the project. *Each member's contribution is important.*

2. Everyone has a job to do. As a group, members should divide and assign tasks necessary to complete the project. Each person is responsible for doing his/her part.

3. Everyone takes turns. Whether sharing ideas or using building materials, group members need to take turns.

4. Everyone shows respect. Everyone has a right to share his/her opinions and ideas without ridicule. If someone disagrees with an idea, that person should point out the weakness in the idea, not in the person who shared it.

2. Block Walk. Familiarize students with the numbering system used on many neighborhood streets: odd numbers on one side of the street, even on the other. (You may want to take another neighborhood walk so students can discover this system for themselves.)

To help students understand the system, place construction paper on the floor in two rows, with one line of masking tape between them. Number the papers on one side of the "street" with odd numbers. Number the others with even numbers. Have most students choose their own "home" and stand on it, and designate several students as workers who might make deliveries in the neighborhood, such as mail carriers, telephone repair workers, and newspaper carriers. Instruct both workers and students to move around the map as you direct them. For example, you might say, "Mail carrier, you have a package to deliver at #9 and a letter to deliver to #12. The mail carrier would then walk to #9, deliver a make-believe parcel, and proceed to #12 to deliver a letter. The mail carrier would then stay there, and the person at #12 might be instructed to visit a friend at #15. In this way, students can move back and forth along the street, reinforcing their understanding of how numbers are used to mark homes and establishments.

If you've made a neighborhood model, invite students to add numbers to their buildings.

MAPS

The ultimate goal of the following activities is to help students recognize the components of a neighborhood as they are shown on a map and to strengthen skills in map reading. To heighten success, you may wish to start with simple mapping activities such as mapping the classroom before moving on to the more abstract concept of mapping neighborhoods. If your students are older and familiar with mapping, however, you may wish to begin with the neighborhood mapping activities.

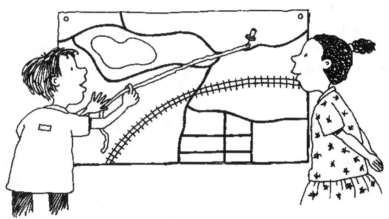

Mapping the Model Neighborhood

Supplies: craft paper, glue, tape, scissors, a map of your school, construction paper, crayons, large index cards, masking tape, drawing paper

If you've made a neighborhood model, making a map of it is a great way to introduce maps. Make the map the same size as the model. Use pieces of paper roughly the same size of the buildings to represent the buildings on your model. Place the map and model alongside one another so kids understand the relationship between the two. Invite students to take turns moving a building on the model, and then moving the corresponding paper on the map.

Extension Activities

1. Make One Big Classroom Map Another way to introduce maps is by making a map of your classroom. Using large pieces of paper to make shapes for desks and other objects in the classroom, help your students create a large map of your classroom on the floor, wall, or bulletin board. Once the map is complete, allow students to make suggestions as to how the room might be rearranged. If possible, carry out some of the changes, then rearrange the map to match. NOTE: Groups of four or five students can work on group maps. They can cut shapes out of construction paper to represent desks, chairs, bookshelves, and so on. Provide a separate sheet of paper for the groups to arrange the shapes on before they glue them down.

2. Tour the School Obtain a floor plan of your school. If possible, create a transparency of it and display it for the class. (Or pass out individual or group copies of the map.) Have students study the map and find key places in the school such as their classroom, the principal's office, the cafeteria, the gymnasium, and so on. Once students are familiar with the layout, challenge them to find places on the map based on clues you provide. For example, you might say, "Whose classroom is three rooms to the left of ours?" or "Give me directions from our classroom to the Main Office." Alternate: Ask students to take a sheet of drawing paper home and draw a map of their own home or, for younger students, their bedroom.

3. Put Them on the Map Have students use their own bodies to make a neighborhood map. Assign each student the role of some structure or location that might be found in a neighborhood, such as a home, apartment building, playground, school, or bus stop. Write the name of that location on a large index card, and tape it on the student. Gather the class together, and allow students to determine where everyone should stand to create the model neighborhood. Homes, for example, might line up in rows on each side of a street. (Streets can be indicated by masking tape placed on the floor.) A bus stop might stand in front of the playground. Adjust the activity as needed; if things seem hectic, you may want to assign some students the job of placing their classmates in the neighborhood rather than leaving this up to class discussion. In addition, some students may want to be people who live in the neighborhood and move around it

Using Community Maps

Supplies: at least four maps of your students' community; yarn, pushpins

This mapping activity will help familiarize your students with reading and understanding a map of their own community.

Divide the class into at least four groups, depending on how many maps you are able to obtain. Provide each group with a map of their community, and spend time explaining how to read the map and helping students to locate some key places in the community, such as their school, a well-known store or restaurant, and possibly even students' own neighborhoods. Depending on the age of your students and their prior experience with map-reading, this preparation

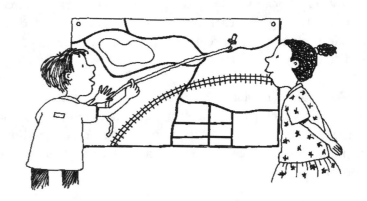

may take minutes or much longer. **NOTE:** If students seem to have excessive difficulty working with the maps, you may want to sketch out a simpler map, create a copy for each student, and complete the activity as a class.

Once students know how to move around the map, ask each group (or work as a class) to plot out a route to get from one location in the community to another. For example, students might show a route from their school to the post office or from the public library to the town hall. Older students might describe the route in words: "Take Main Street to Parker Avenue. Turn left onto Parker Avenue and travel until Wise Street...." Younger students might simply trace the route with their finger when asked.

NOTE: For whole-class activities, pin a community map to a bulletin board in your classroom. Pin one end of a length of yarn to a location on the map, then use the yarn to mark the route from that place to another specified location. Secure the yarn in place with pushpins as needed.

Extension Activities

1. Where To Go for What You Need Share with your students Marjorie Priceman's *How To Make an Apple Pie and See the World* (Knopf, 1994). In this story, a young girl embarks on a

worldwide trip one evening to find the ingredients she needs to make an apple pie. Take your students beyond the story by asking them where they would go to find similar ingredients in or near their own community. Encourage students not to rely wholly on a supermarket for their supplies, but to consider the origin of each item. Apples, for example, can be picked from an orchard, while butter can be churned on a dairy farm. You may wish to add extra challenge by asking students to bring in simple recipes from home and conduct the same activity for each, or place a variety of recipes in a learning center to serve as a free-time activity.

2. Mystery Location Have students take turns reading directions to "mystery locations" on their community map. Ask each student to write step-by-step directions for getting from a specific location to another that remains a mystery until classmates follow the directions, trace the route, and determine the location.

3. Community Regions Ask older students to study a community map and divide it into regions: In which part of the community does most government work take place? In which part of town are most schools, recreation facilities, churches, homes, shops, or restaurants? In some communities, divisions will be obvious and easy to make; in others, there will be no clear division by region.

4. Draw Your Own Route Provide students with crayons and drawing paper, and ask each student to draw the route s/he takes to get from home to school. Younger students may want to draw from memory as they believe the route exists, noting landmarks along the way such as schools or other buildings passed, bodies of water passed, and so on. Older students may wish to refer to the map for a more exact replication of their route.

5. My Favorite Place Ask students to answer the following questions by writing, drawing, or both: "What is your favorite place in the community, and why do you like it best?"

Bookshelf

The Whole World in Your Hands: Looking at Maps by Melvin Berger and Gilda Berger (Discovery Readers, 1993) A book for beginning readers that introduces many different kinds of maps.

Puzzle Maps U.S.A. by Nancy Clouse (Henry Holt, 1990) A playful approach to maps in which the shapes of states are combined in new ways.

As the Crow Flies: A First Book of Maps by Gail Hartman (Macmillan, 1991) A wonderful introduction to the concept of maps through the environments of various animals.

Globes by Paul Sipiera (New True Books, 1991) An introduction to the various types of globes, what they represent, and their history.

Model Community: People and Transportation

TIP! Cut along dashed lines and fold along solid lines.

Model Community: Buildings

Model Community: Buildings

Model Community: Buildings

Communities Grow and Change

Part 3

Communities can change in many ways: they can get smaller or bigger; deteriorate or improve; respond to changes in economics or demographics. In this section students examine some of the ways communities, including their own, change and the reasons for those changes.

COMMUNITIES CHANGE

New Providence: A Changing Cityscape by Renata von Tschamer and Ronald Lee Fleming (Gulliver Books, 1987)
Students explore the development and deterioration of a fictional community over the course of 80 years.

Before Reading
Discuss changes that have happened in your community with your students. Are there any new buildings? Have any stores closed? Has a local playground been upgraded? Tell students you are going to read them a book that tells about the changes in one city called New Providence. Explain that although New Providence is fictional, the authors used authentic details from old photographs of various towns across the country.

After Reading
Talk about what life must have been like for the inhabitants of New Providence in 1910. What types of homes did they live in? What kind of clothing did they wear? What were the methods of transportation? Make a list as students cite details. For older students, divide the class into pairs or small groups and assign each group one category such as clothing, population, architecture, or transportation. Ask them to look at details in each picture from 1910 to 1987 that show the changes over time in their category. Younger students may track changes in a section of the illustrations, such as the park in the foreground, the countryside behind the town, or one of the buildings. Have students share their findings with the class.

Extension Activities

1. Keep a Journal Have students pretend they are visiting New Providence in 1910. Ask older students to write an entry in a travel diary or a letter to a loved one back home, describing what they have seen or done in the town. Younger students may draw pictures of what they have seen for a travel diary.

2. Signs of the Times Ask students to take a closer look at the signs on buildings advertising products and businesses. Discuss which of these might be around today, or if changing public taste or need has decreased the popularity of these goods and services. Have students create advertisements for things they enjoy using or doing today, such as running shoes, outdoor activities, foods, and so on. Encourage students to think of creative advertisements, such as they might hear on the radio or see on television. Commercials might be performed for the class, and signs can be displayed around the classroom.

3. Maintaining the Community Have students look at the park in the book which is in the foreground of the illustration for 1980. Ask them to compare it to the setting in 1935. How has the area changed? Which do they think would be a nicer area to spend time in? Then look at the illustration for 1987. Discuss how an area might fall apart and how it might be improved. (For example: people might neglect the litter and graffiti, making it a less inviting area. Cleaning the area would encourage people to stay.) Have students brainstorm ways to prevent an area from deteriorating. Then ask them if there are any areas in their community which might benefit from such suggestions.

Our Community Over Time

Supplies: current and historic photos of your students' community

Students explore primary sources to learn about their own community's past as well as to make comparisons of life there long ago and today.

Provide your students with photographs of their community from the past and present. You may be able to borrow these from a local historical society, the public library, or the Office of the Town or City Clerk. Divide the class into small groups, and provide each group with some photographs to compare. Have students note similarities and differences between their community

past and present. Have them write down their observations or discuss them as a class and create a chart comparing life and landmarks then and now.

As students study the photographs and maps, guide them with questions such as:

- What do you see in the photographs from long ago that you see in this community today? What do you see that is different?
- Were there more or fewer buildings/homes/trees/fields long ago?
- Are the changes you see due to people or nature (tornadoes, erosion, construction, etc.)?
- What changes or similarities do you notice in the way people dress?
- How have the boundaries of our community changed/stayed the same since long ago?
- What was the land like where your neighborhood/a shopping mall/our school is now? Was it once a grassy field? A forest?

Extension Activities

1. Visiting Historians Invite members of your local historical society to share historical aspects of your own community with your class. Topics of interest might include the year the community was founded, the oldest residences, streets, and places of business, as well as symbols of the town and traditions started long ago that exist today. Encourage older students to ask questions and jot down notes as the visitors speak. For younger students, you might make a list of facts on chart paper. You might also consider a walking field trip for all students to point out some of the places named by the historians. Encourage students to make comparisons of old and new photographs of places and sites named.

2. Senior Interviews Give your students a chance to learn about history from people who have experienced it firsthand: Seniors! Invite longtime community residents into your classroom to talk with your students about life in the community long ago. Encourage seniors to bring in photographs and mementos and to share stories with your students. **NOTE:** To make the best use of class time, encourage students to prepare questions for the seniors before they arrive. Questions might include:

- What games did you like to play?
- Where did you go to school?
- Where did you shop?
- What was your favorite toy?
- How was our town/city different from what it is today?
- How was our town/city the same as it is today?

3. Who's Who in the Community? Have students choose a noted person who lives or lived in your community and learn more about that person's life. Older students may write a brief biography including details about the person's childhood, family, likes and dislikes, and accomplishments. Younger children may draw a picture illustrating why that person is well known. Compile the biographies into one class book. Then photocopy the book and give copies to students. **NOTE:** Students may substitute a senior citizen or family member for their profiles.

4. (Your Community) 2020 As students learn about their community's past, start them thinking about the future. Have them brainstorm what goals their community might have or changes they think might take place in the future. What might school be like in twenty years? What type of clothing might they be wearing? What methods of transportation might be available? Older students may write about what they think should improve in their community. Young students may draw a picture of what they imagine the future to be like in their community. Students' work might be displayed in a community center, school, or local library.

BOOKSTOP

Home Place by Crescent Dragonwagon (Macmillan, 1990)
This literature selection helps students to discover that small trinkets left behind can provide insight to life in the past.

Before Reading

Talk with your students about leaving things behind. Ask them to think of times when they've gone on a picnic or off to a friend's house with a special toy or possession and then forgotten to take it with them when they left. If the item was never retrieved, chances are that it was found by someone else or will eventually be found by someone else. Explain that sometimes, this is how people learn about those who came before them. When they see what is left behind, it tells them a little bit about someone else. This is especially meaningful if the item found is very old, giving insight not only into another life but into another time period as well.

After Reading

Have students talk about things they have "uncovered" in their home or backyard, giving some insight into the person or persons who lived there before they did. Perhaps they came across small toys hidden in the lawn or old tools that were left in a shed or garage. Or maybe they found old clothing or letters in an attic or basement. What did they learn from the items they found?

When students have shared their experiences, talk about other discoveries that can teach about the past. In addition to finding objects, people can observe details in their environment. Cracked paint or torn wallpaper can reveal older layers underneath. Imprints of hands, feet, or signatures in cement walkways show who was present when the cement was wet. And flower bulbs that bloom every year reveal someone's hard work just as old stone walls do; someone had to place them there by hand.

Over the next several days, ask your students to look for signs of the past in their homes, school, and neighborhood. Urge them to take notes about what they observe and share their observations with the class. Younger students may want to draw a picture of something they have found or seen from the past.

Extension Activities

1. Make a Time Capsule Help your students create a time capsule intended for students in the same grade ten years from now. Use a large plastic storage box as a capsule. Help your students fill the box with items they feel best represent their class. These might include samples of work they have done, illustrations or magazine cut-outs of popular toys they like to play with and clothing they wear, "book reports" of favored books they enjoy reading, and letters from your students to students ten years from now, telling about their lives, their interests, and life in the community this year. Unless you prefer to keep the box in your own home, check with your school principal to see where it might best be stored to ensure it will be found and opened ten years from now.

2. Write a Story Invite your students to pretend they are an item that someone left behind at a picnic, a ball game, or some other event. Help them write a fiction story to describe the chain of events that would happen to them next. For example, a toy dinosaur left under a tree at the park might be found by a child who takes it home. Days later, the child takes the dinosaur to the beach and buries it in the sand, where it is once again forgotten, and then found by someone else. Older students may be able to write their own short stories. Younger students may work together with you to write one as a class.

Bookshelf

Visiting a Village by Bobbie Kalman (Crabtree, 1990) The author explains what life is like long ago in a historic American community.

The Potato Man by Megan McDonald (Orchard Books, 1991) A grandfather tells the story of his childhood when a peddler sold fruits and vegetables in the neighborhood.

The Legend of New Amsterdam by Peter Spier (Doubleday, 1979) A story about New York City and its history.

Heron Street by Ann Turner (Harper, 1989) This book details changes in an area from pre-colonial days to the present.

My Backyard History Book by David Weitzman (Little, Brown, 1975) What's the best way to learn about your community's past? Get out there and look! The author offers page after page of activities and tips to help young and old learn about the rich heritage within their community—through interviews, field trips, observations, and more.

Being Part of a Community

Part 4

As students recognize that changes in a community affect its members, they also begin to realize that what members of the community do will have an impact on the community as a whole. In Part Four, students explore their potential for contributing to the community.

PEOPLE MAKE A DIFFERENCE

Miss Rumphius by Barbara Cooney (Viking, 1982)
In this delightful story students identify the contributions of one individual and examine things they can do to make their own community a better place to live in.

Before Reading

Ask students to imagine what the world would be like if no one took care of the environment, planted flowers, disposed properly of litter, or recycled bottles and cans. Help them realize that without people's help and concern, the environment would suffer deeply and would eventually become an unpleasant place to live. Ask students to name things people do in their community to beautify or better the community in some way. Perhaps old buildings have just been replaced or remodeled. Perhaps a run-down park was recently landscaped and made beautiful with flowers and trees.

After Reading

Talk with your students about Miss Rumphius' contribution to the community: the flowers she planted which brightened and beautified the landscape long after she lived. Explain that people of all ages and in all parts of the world can do something to make a difference in their community. They might do something for the environment, such as planting flowers and trees. They might do something for others, such as operating a soup kitchen or caring for stray animals.

Invite your students to think about something they might do in their lifetime to contribute to their current or future community in some way. It need not be something immediate; it could happen fifty or more years from now. The timing is not important; the vision is.

Provide younger students with drawing paper and crayons. Ask them to draw themselves doing something to make a difference in the world. Ask older students to describe in writing what they would like to do for the world or community and then illustrate it.

Extension Activities

1. Find Related Stories Ask students to search their school, local, or home libraries for picture books or chapter books that tell of people caring for their community in some way. Encourage each student to bring one book to school and tell the class about the story and how the character(s) contributed to the community.

2. Make a Community Contributor's Quilt Ask students to talk with their families, neighbors, and anyone they know in the community to learn about people who have made notable contributions to the community. Using muslin and fabric crayons (or squares of craft paper and markers/crayons/paints), have each student illustrate one square in honor of a community contributor. Students can design their own squares, but each one should feature the contributor's name as well as an illustration of their contribution.

3. Five Fingers for the Community Have each student trace his/her hand on a sheet of paper. Within each traced finger, have the student write or draw one way s/he can contribute to the community.

4. Write a Fairy Tale or Folk Tale Encourage your students to write a tale about someone who moved into a community and changed that community forever. The story may be set in the present day or long ago and may take place anywhere in the world.

Emma's Day Off (A Read-Aloud Play)

Reading or performing this play is a great way to illustrate how members of a community depend on one another. It has eight main speaking parts, but everyone can participate by being townspeople. The play can be read or you may do a more formal production with costumes, props, and sound effects. For children who aren't readers yet, you may want to read the play, but have children pantomime the actions.

Emma's Day Off
by Kathleen M. Hollenbeck

Characters
Narrator
Emma McGee
Robert Cly
Joe Ricco
Melva
Dr. Mendoza
Geraldine Jenkes
Grace Reed
Townspeople

ACT 1

SETTING: The Post Office in the town of Homebody, U.S.A.

NARRATOR: It's six-thirty in the morning. Mail carrier Emma McGee arrives at the Homebody Post Office.

EMMA: (Trying to unlock the door with a key. She sighs and leans against the door.) Every day it's the same. Work, work, work, and never enough rest. Well, I'm tired. I think I'll take the day off.

(Emma takes out a large sheet of paper and a marker. In big letters, she writes POST OFFICE CLOSED TODAY. Emma hangs the sign on the door and walks offstage, yawning.)

NARRATOR: At eight o'clock, the first customer arrives.

ROBERT CLY: (Reading sign) Post Office closed today? How can the Post Office be closed? I have important letters to mail!

(Robert Cly looks around in frustration. He is carrying a large bundle of letters.)

ROBERT CLY: This is terribly inconvenient!

JOE RICCO: (Approaching) What's going on?

ROBERT CLY: The Post Office is closed for the day, and I can't mail my letters. I have bills to pay, and they must be delivered on time!

JOE RICCO: I have a package to mail. If I don't mail it today, it will arrive late for my grandmother's birthday. How can I mail it with the Post Office closed?

ROBERT CLY: Let's look around town. Someone must know how to open the Post Office.

ACT 2

SETTING: Melva's General Store

MELVA: (Checking her watch.) It's almost nine, and the mail hasn't come yet! Emma McGee always brings my mail first. She knows I need my supplies first thing in the morning. My customers will be here, wanting their orders filled. I'll have to turn them away!

NARRATOR: Just then, Dr. Mendoza, Homebody Veterinarian, comes into the store.

DR. MENDOZA: (Smiling) Morning, Melva. Got the medicine I ordered last week?

MELVA: I'm sorry, Dr. Mendoza. I had to special order that medicine. It was supposed to be here today, but the mail hasn't come yet.

DR. MENDOZA: A sick dog, two cats, and a pig are on their way to my office right now. They need that medicine right away!

MELVA: I understand, Dr. Mendoza. I'll bring it to your office myself when it arrives.

(Dr. Mendoza leaves. Geraldine Jenkes, the town hair dresser, enters.)

GERALDINE JENKES: Hi, Melva. I've come to pick up the case of shampoo I ordered. And just in time, too. I used up my last bottle yesterday!

MELVA: I wish I could help you, but the mail is late. Your shampoo isn't here yet.

GERALDINE JENKES: (shocked) But I need it! Without shampoo, I can't wash my customers' hair. I'll lose business! I have four customers coming in today to get ready for a wedding. What will I do?

MELVA: I'll call you when it comes in. That's the best I can do.

(Geraldine Jenkes storms out of the store. Grace Reed walks in.)

GRACE REED: Good morning, Melva. I've come to pick up the inflatable raft I ordered.

MELVA: Your raft is not here yet. The mail is late, and I don't know when it will arrive.

GRACE REED: I'm leaving for a ten-day rafting trip this afternoon! I can't go without a raft!

MELVA: When the mail comes, I'll call you.

(Grace begins to protest. At this time, the door opens and Robert Cly enters with Joe Ricco.)

JOE RICCO: I'm visiting from out of town. Can anyone tell me who runs the Post Office here?

MELVA: Emma McGee. Why do you ask?

JOE RICCO: We have letters and packages to mail, but the Post Office is closed.

MELVA and GRACE: (Together) How can the Post Office be closed?

ROBERT CLY: There's a sign on the door. It says the Post Office is closed today. The doors are locked, and there's no one to take or deliver the mail.

MELVA: My customers are waiting for important packages to arrive! Animals are waiting for their medicine! Customers are counting on shampoo!

GRACE: I'll have to postpone my vacation.

ROBERT CLY: It's an inconvenience to us all. My bills will be late, and this will cost me a great deal of money.

JOE RICCO: My gift will be late, and my grandmother will think I forgot.

ROBERT CLY: Do you know where to find Emma McGee?

MELVA: She lives on the Bricklewood Farm.

GRACE: Let's go!

(The whole group leaves the store.)

ACT 3

SETTING: The cottage of Emma McGee.

NARRATOR: As Melva and the others walk toward Emma's home, more townspeople join them. People wanting to send or receive postcards, packages, letters, and tickets follow along. By the time they reach Emma's, there are more than 30 people in the group.

(Melva knocks on Emma's front door. After a while, a sleepy Emma opens the door. She is shocked to see the large crowd standing before her.)

EMMA: Oh my goodness! What's going on?

DR. MENDOZA: The Post Office is closed.

ROBERT CLY: No one can mail letters or packages.

MELVA: No one can receive any, either.

GRACE: Some of us are waiting for important deliveries.

JOE RICCO: How can you close the Post Office when so many of us are depending on you?

EMMA: I was so tired! I thought Homebody could get along without me for one day.

MELVA: We can't get along without you!

ROBERT CLY: Will you please take down the sign and open the Post Office today?

GERALDINE JENKES: We know you work hard, Emma. You do need a rest.

DR. MENDOZA: We'll hold a town meeting tomorrow. We'll hire someone to help you with the mail.

TOWNSPEOPLE: Yes, yes! We'll hire a helper for Emma!

EMMA: (Smiling.) That would really be great.

MELVA: Will you come back today? Please?

EMMA: I'm on my way!

(Dressed in pajamas, Emma steps outside and begins walking down the road with the townspeople. As the scene ends, she can be heard talking with them.)

EMMA: Now who has things to mail? And who's waiting for packages? Dr. Mendoza, your medicine came in last night. And Grace, your raft is taking up half my office. That must be some vacation you're planning...

THE END

Good for the Community Poster

Supplies: craft paper, markers, magazine pictures

This poster-making activity allows students to explore ways people positively and negatively affect a community.

Talk with your students about what it means to be a member of a community. Explain that every member of the community can affect the community in some way, be it a good way or a bad way. With the class, list ways people affect their community, both positively and negatively. (See the sample chart below.)

Ways People Help the Community

volunteering
recycling
taking care of own home and property
donating money to help the needy
conserving water and fuel
visiting the sick or elderly

Ways People Hurt the Community

wasting fuel, water, or electricity
littering
destroying property
not keeping home or property clean
caring only about themselves and their needs
stealing

Have students create a poster showing one way people can either help or hurt the community. They may draw pictures or make a collage from magazines. Display the posters around the school or at community centers. Younger students may work as a class or in groups.

Extension Activities

1. Honor People Who Help the Community Designate wall space or a bulletin board in your classroom or corridor to post photographs or illustrations of people who deserve recognition for their help in the community.

Ask each student to focus on one person whom they feel has truly helped the community in some way. Younger students may draw a picture of this person and write/dictate the person's name and a brief description of what that person has done to deserve recognition. Older students may be able to track down photographs of their subjects and write a paragraph telling why that person should be recognized as someone who helps the community.

2. Make Thank-You Cards Allow each child to choose one person whom they feel helps the community in an important way. Provide drawing paper, markers and crayons, scissors, glue, glitter, and other craft materials. Have each student make a card to say "Thank You" to the community helper they've chosen.

3. We Are Helpers! Help your students realize that every contribution, no matter how small, is appreciated and helpful to a community. Invite your students to share stories about helpful things they have done recently. Have each student draw a picture of himself/herself doing the helpful deed and then write/dictate sentences describing the deed and how it affected others.

4. Read All About It! Help your students write an ad for the Help Wanted section of a community newspaper. Have each student write and illustrate one entry for the column, citing the need for someone to perform a helpful task or action that works for the good of the community, such as: "Neat person wanted to put litter in trash cans."

RESOLVING DIFFERENCES IN THE COMMUNITY

The Troubled Village by Simon Henwood (Farrar, Straus and Giroux, 1991)
In this lighthearted story, the people of Troubed Village like to disagree. When the sky falls in, they finally learn how to resolve conflicts.

Before Reading
Help your students identify things people do when they disagree. Begin the discussion by asking why people might disagree with each other or fight. For example, people sometimes disagree when:

- two people want the same toy or other object.
- someone refuses to share.
- two people want to be first.
- one person leaves another to clean up a mess they both made.
- a big job needs to be done and no one wants to do it.

Ask your students what they do when involved in a conflict or disagreement with someone else. List their responses on the board.

Explain that today you will share a story about an entire community of people who did not get along and who needed to find a way to work together.

After Reading

Provide drawing paper and crayons. Have students create comic strips about a real or imagined neighborhood conflict, illustrating the conflict and a positive resolution. Have younger students draw only one scene rather than a whole comic strip. Encourage them to illustrate either the conflict or its resolution and to dictate one or two sentences of explanation. For added challenge: You may wish to have older students draw only the first several frames of the comic strip, depicting the conflict without a resolution. When students have finished, collect the comic strips and distribute them at random. Have classmates complete each others' comic strips with peaceful and positive resolutions.

Extension Activities

1. Community Skits Divide the class into groups of four to six students. Allow time for each group to create and present its own skit about a neighborhood conflict and its resolution. You may wish to provide each group with a specific situation of conflict, described on an index card, or you may wish to use the following conflicts:

> **A.** Mr. Barnes and Ms. Timpo are neighbors. Their homes are side by side. Their backyards are separated by a row of tall pine trees. Mr. Barnes wants to cut the trees down to allow more sunlight to come into his yard. Ms. Timpo wants to keep the trees there, as a fence between the two yards.
>
> **B.** Jim lives in an apartment building. He likes to listen to loud music all day and late at night. Jim's neighbors can hear the loud music. They have asked Jim politely to turn the music down. Jim enjoys his music. He doesn't want to turn it down.
>
> **C.** Nancy lives in a large neighborhood. Most of her neighbors work hard to keep their homes and their lawns looking nice. Nancy works at a hospital six days a week. She has very little time to take care of her home or property. Nancy's neighbors feel that her yard looks messy and is making the neighborhood look bad.
>
> **D.** Mr. Morgan lives in a house across the street from a brand new ball field. Every night, bright lights from the ball field shine into Mr. Morgan's home. Mr. Morgan cannot sleep with the lights shining into his home.

2. Create a Caring Classroom Poster To help your students remember to keep their classroom a caring one, work together to create a poster telling how a conflicts can be peacefully resolved. Elicit suggestions from your students, and then write on a large piece of poster paper. The list might include suggestions such as:

- Try to talk out the problem.
- Think of ways to satisfy everyone involved.
- Ask an adult or a friend to help solve the dispute.
- Spend time apart for a while.

Be a Community Star

Supplies: A copy of pages 53-55, scissors, dice, coins or squares of paper (for playing pieces)
Object: This game challenges students to think of the many ways they can help others in their own community.
Players: 2-4

Reproduce pages 53-55 for your students. Have them cut the game cards on the lines and place them on the game board. Have students read the directions and play the game in groups of two to four.

This game challenges students to think of the many ways they can help others in their own community. Students can play the game in pairs or small groups. Reproduce page 55 for each student. Also make a double-sided photocopy of pages 53 and 54 for each pair or group. Have each pair or group cut out their star cards.

Each player should choose a different coin or a different colored square of paper as a playing piece. Invite each player to roll the die, and then move his or her playing piece the number of spaces shown on it. If the playing piece lands on a star, the student reads, or you can read, a star card.

The questions on the game cards can be answered in different ways. Use the questions and the students' answers as an opportunity to explore ways people can help in a community. Accept reasonable answers that students give to the questions posed. **NOTE:** This is also an opportunity to discuss safety issues. Be sure to emphasize that children should always talk to a parent or guardian before attempting to help anyone. When a star card question is answered, the student gets to keep the card. When a student gets three cards, they get to be Community Stars and wear the star badge found at the bottom of page 55.

Extension Activities

1. Helping in Our Community Use the phone book to find organizations and groups that provide help in your community. You may wish to create a chart to identify each organization, its function, and the benefits of its works. (See sample chart below.) Ask students why they think it's important to have such groups in the community.

Organization	What It Does	How It Helps
American Red Cross	Provides food, shelter, and other basic supplies in time of need, usually due to natural disasters or wartime difficulties.	Saves lives; provides for basic human needs; improves quality of life after a disaster or difficulty or after wartime.
Soup Kitchen	Provides food for needy people.	Provides healthful and usually hot meals.
Homeless Shelter	Provides shelter for people who have no home to go to.	Saves lives; provides a clean and comfortable environment.

2. Make a Community Pledge Give each student one copy of the Community Pledge certificate on page 56. Have each student think of one positive action s/he could carry out to improve or contribute to the community in some way. Have each student write or dictate a sentence describing that action and then illustrate themselves carrying it out. To assist students in choosing and making their pledges, you might brainstorm as a class to come up with a list of things people can do to help strengthen, improve, or contribute to their community. Examples include:

- Weed a home garden.
- Walk a neighbor's dog.
- Rake up leaves and brush.
- Sweep sidewalks.
- Shovel snow.
- Visit an elderly, sick, or lonely friend or neighbor (with permission of parent/guardian).
- Pick up litter and put it in a trash can.

- Help plant flowers as part of a neighborhood/community improvement effort.
- Do one kind thing for another person each day (or week).
- Donate toys/food/clothing to the needy.
- Volunteer time at a soup kitchen.
- Start a penpal exchange with someone in a community far away.

Keep a classroom or schoolwide graph of community service actions, detailing the jobs students have done and the time they have spent. Be sure to hold a Volunteer Appreciation Ceremony (or a Free Time Festival for Volunteers) to reward and thank the children for their time, effort, and contributions.

Bookshelf

City Green by DyAnne DiSalvo-Ryan (Morrow Junior Books, 1994) This is a heartwarming story about neighbors working together to beautify a vacant lot.

Sam Johnson and the Blue Ribbon Quilt by Lisa Campbell Ernst (Lothrop, 1983) When a competition gets down to the wire, the men and women in a community learn that the best way to win is by working together.

Garden of Dreams by Richard M. Wainwright (Family Life Publishing, 1994) Best-suited for

older readers, this story tells of a boy's dream to improve his urban neighborhood and of the children who give life to his dream.

Old Henry by Joan Blos (Morrow, 1987) Old Henry moves out of the community when his neighbors aren't willing to accept the way he maintains his property.

Stop Your Crowing, Kasimir! by Ursel Scheffler (Carolrhoda Books, 1988) When neighbors complain about a rooster's wake-up call, they come to regret their whining.

Be a Community Star!
(Game Cards)

Be a Community Star!
(Game Cards)

You notice the water fountain at the playground is leaking. What can you do to help?	It is daytime. You see a raccoon wandering around the school playground. What can you do to help?	A boy in your school is very sick. His family needs money to pay hospital bills. What can you do to help?
You visit the park with your family. You see a lot of litter on the ground. What can you do to help?	You are riding your bike home from a friend's house. You see smoke rising from a barn on the side of the road. What can you do to help?	A neighbor of yours has just moved into a nursing home. He is lonely and feeling sad. What can you do to help?
You are at the store with your dad. You see a small child by herself. She is crying and seems to be lost. What can you do to help?	You watched the news last night. You learned there are people in your community who do not have enough food to eat. What can you do to help?	A neighbor of yours cannot see very well. You see her walking down the sidewalk. You know the sidewalk is icy. What can you do to help?
Your family uses lots of cans, bottles, and paper. You want to cut down on the amount of trash your family makes. What can you do to help?	Your friend stays alone after school while her dad works. Sometimes your friend feels lonely by herself. What can you do to help?	It is fall. Lots of leaves have begun to fall. Your neighbor has a broken leg and can't rake her yard. What can you do to help?

Be a Community Star!
(Game Board)

Put your playing piece on any circle. Roll the die and move around the board. Pick a card when you land on a star. Read the card aloud and answer the question by telling how a community helper would solve the problem. After you answer, keep the star card. When you get three star cards, you become a **Community Star!**

Place Cards Here

COMMUNITY STAR

My Community Pledge

I pledge to help my community by doing this:

_____

_____

_____

_____

_____   _____
Student's Signature   Teacher's Signature